Holy Ghost Drive By
Vol 1: Fully Loaded

Sharpshooter Jerri P. Beasley

Ignited Ink 717
2020

Copyright © 2020 Jerri P Beasley

All rights reserved. This book or any portion thereof may not be re-produced or used in any manner whatsoever without the express written permission of the publisher except for the use of brief quotations in a book review or scholarly journal.

First Printing: 2020

ISBN 978-1-7352286-2-4

www.JBProductions.work

Ignited Ink 717

IgnitedInk717@gmail.com

@IgnitedInk717

Cover Photography By Ferrell E. Phelps

Author Hairstylist: Myra L. Jackson

Dedication

This book is dedicated to the loving
memory of my
Warrior Woman,
Verdell Beasley. I love and appreciate you,
Momma!!!!

Acknowledgments

I thank God for all the loving support and guidance that I've had along this journey called life.

First and foremost, to my Lord and Savior Jesus Christ who truly looked past all my faults and saw my needs, He turned me around, I'm forever grateful. To my natural Late Father, David Joseph Beasley, who I get a lot of my quick wit from and the visionary mindset. He instilled in me early to be proud of who I was and never half step.

To my loving Late Mother, Verdell Beasley, who was and still is 'the wind beneath my wings', the one who told me to soar when I was at my lowest, the one who picked me up with her words and unconditional love. She saw in me everything the enemy tried to blind me from seeing. When she left this earth my heart was crushed.

My spirit is lifted knowing her love for me was the realest and she would never have left me if God didn't make her an offer she couldn't refuse. Who could be mad at that?

I love you, Momma with all that is in me, and I'm determined to stay the course so I can see you again!

To my sister Rhondalyn, you are my second mom, a true supporter and protector. You have always cheered me on from the sidelines and made sure I was good! Momma said it was just the two of us, but I know we have all of Heaven backing us up. There is nothing we can not accomplish. Love you Big Sis!

To Attorney Ben Hall and Sandra Hall, thank you for the platform and the trust. We were brought together by God and you both have been a sense of strength and family for me. I am grateful for our paths crossing.

To my publisher, Ebony Rose of Ignited Ink 717, thank you for hearing the voice of God concerning me. HGDB book, has always been a thought, but you put the legs to it, and I'm grateful.

To every friend, foe, supporter, and non supporter I thank you as well, for all have given me what was needed to do every Holy Ghost Drive-By, I am grateful.

PREFACE

Buckle up and follow the Holy Ghost to a better destination. Start each day gearing up reading your devotional. Before your day can take a left turn, Lock &Load. We are aiming at everything hindering us from being all that God wants us to be!

x

Introduction

Holy Ghost Drive By, real and revealing.

The Holy Ghost Drive By is my conversations with the Lord. His private responses that I choose to make public. Just in case you needed to hear it too!

People have asked me, "Are you talking about me in your drive bys?"

My answer: "If you had to ask, it is likely you are one of the ones He was aiming at. Lol."

I often say I was the first to get shot, so no shade intended. Just get under His shelter if convicted.

I thank God for those who have said the Drive Bys have helped them or confirmed what they have been told, I also thank God for those who have been bothered by them, it hasn't stopped you from reading and discussing them, so any press is good press.

Lord willing, the Holy Ghost Drive Bys will continue to roll on, aiming to uplift, enlighten and frustrate the plans of the enemy! I pray the blessings of God over all of you.

Holy Ghost Drive By  Day 1

One person said something at Aretha Franklin's funeral that really stuck with me. He said that Aretha made her presence known!

She used her platform to go far beyond it being about her. It was about others. Many said that Aretha took them places they would have never gone in order to teach them lessons they would have never learned.

Question: Is your presence known when you show up and missed when you are gone?
Is your platform all about you or is it to pull up, educate, and
introduce others to what will make them better?
All the singing, wardrobe changes,
and invited guests did not stick out
to me more than the statement.

She Made Her Presence Known!

We are here for a short time. He said He'll make our
name great, but it is up to us to Make our presence
known by being truly present in the lives of others.
Not for fame, fortune or notoriety
but because the spirit of God in us
to be felt by others.

I'm determine to make my presence
known by being in His presence.

Lock & Load

Tips on Getting into God's Presence

- Set aside time JUST for God.
- Silence your phone.
- Call Out to Him.
- Find a nice worship mix. (kcohradio.com)
- How will you be present in the life of someone else today?

Holy Ghost Drive By  Day 2

They plotted it, but He is going to block it.
They thought you were just nice.
They did not know you were anointed and covered.
The enemy is about to find out he picked the wrong one to try and mess over.
The season of getting over on you has ended.
Whoever tries it, will wish they did right by you.
Stay in the safety of His will.
Your doing right, even when done wrong, is about to pay off. Nothing has been overlooked or wasted.

Lock & Load

What is an instance where you turned the other cheek? Took the high road? Let that joker make it?

What does "stay in the safety of His will" mean to you?

Holy Ghost Drive By  Day 3

If they are Blind to your victory moments when they are not in the picture, they are not your friends!!

They are opportunists waiting for a photo opp!!

BE DONE
with *fictitious fellowship* and make room for
divine partnerships!
They will be excited about your excitement, whether the flash caught their good side or not!

Lock & Load

Is there anyone in your group picture who should be cropped out?

Is there anyone at your last celebration who did not say, *"hooray?"*

During your next victory, pay attention to see who does not clap.

Holy Ghost Drive By  Day 4

When God gives you true discernment, do not allow yourself or others to convince you that you are being paranoid.
In this phase of your journey,
remember what you learned from ignoring the signs.
If it appears too good to be true, it normally is.
Even a good thing with wrong intentions becomes a bad thing with a plan.
Not every move is to be shared.
Not every granted opportunity for you always equals an opportunity for them.
Visionary keep building, but always keep an eye on your supplies.
The enemy always sends decoys to make sure you come up short

Lock & Load

What is discernment?

What are your supplies?

Holy Ghost Drive By  Day 5

You were not considered a factor because it didn't appear you were even in the race.
You were not at the *"Who's Who"* events. You were not on a flyer everyday. You did not post pics of you hanging out with celebrities. All you were doing was working in the field, being consistent to the assignment, rebuking the desire to quit!
You showed up when others walked out.
You gave when you were not given.

Now is the time!
Last shall be first, and the first shall be last.
You are being requested to sit at the table, where you have never been invited. Do not bring a plus one.
This one is for you! You paid the price to enjoy it
Unapologetically!

Lock & Load

Which field have you been sowing into?

What does your moment of victory look like?

Holy Ghost Drive By  Day 6

For every God-ordained assignment and vision, there is an unseen scanner checking everything that *approaches* or *attaches*. Motives matter to God and He will not allow them to be hidden. If you consult Him He will always reveal them. Don't be afraid or thrown off by what you see now. The mouth is saying one thing, but the face is showing another.
He will not leave you unaware.

Open eyes don't always *see*. Twenty-twenty vision is granted when we sincerely request *sight*.

Faith is blind, but discernment sees clearly.

Lock & Load

Write a prayer asking God to sharpen your discernment and to give you the wisdom to handle what you see.

Holy Ghost Drive By 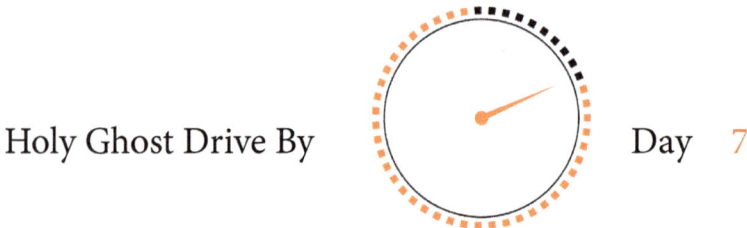 Day 7

This disconnection notice is not coming from the light
company, but straight from God.
Don't find it strange
that some connections
are being disconnected. This is not a bad thing but a
necessary thing.
Do not try and reconnect what
He has disconnected;
it will not work without the power!

Lock & Load

Which one of your connections has an overdue pink slip?

TARGET  PRACTICE

Release

What mindset, habit, or/characteristic did you release this week?

Discernment

Discernment is powerful. We are privileged to see a glimpse of the enemy's plans and have a fair advantage. What has your discernment shown you?

Fear

What scriptures will you shoot at fear this week?

Holy Ghost Drive By  Day 8

You will outlast your enemy if you do not become one. Do not emulate the ways of what you hate.
Do the opposite of what wrong has been done to you.
God will *publicly* honor you because of what you chose to do *privately*.
They schemed; you prayed. They set traps; you opened doors. They excluded; you included. They spoke curses; you spoke blessings.

Never think doing what is right when done wrong is weak. It is truly the strongest position you could take. Humble yourself under the mighty hand of God.
Resist the devil, and he will flee.
In due season, He will exalt you.

Lock & Load

Describe a moment you could have retailiated, but chose to walk out Matthew 5:44

Holy Ghost Drive By  Day 9

Just Heard: If people you love can only be happy for your blessings when they are partakers of your blessings, then they are not supporters but spies. They will show up only to see what they can latch on to.

Do not waste another minute entertaining illegal attachments. Be bold enough to ask God to sever everything or everyone who is illegally attached to you. Do not drag contaminates into your new environment

Lock & Load

Just in case last week the spy wasn't dealt with, follow this checklist to help you:

- ☐ Discussion declaring disconnect
- ☐ Unfollow on Social Media
- ☐ Delete number and text thread
- ☐ Delete any pictures/videos out of your phone
- ☐ Discard any gifts (yes even that one)

Holy Ghost Drive By  Day 10

Visionary leader: Do not settle with having many attached to you. Wait until He sends those assigned to you. When He does, do not allow the *attached* to attack them.

The attached will always fight dirty for their perceived position, but the *assigned* did not come for a position. They came to advance the mission. Know the difference between *attached* and *assigned*. Not knowing could be costly!

Lock & Load

Survey the people in your life who act as if you owe them something?

Holy Ghost Drive By 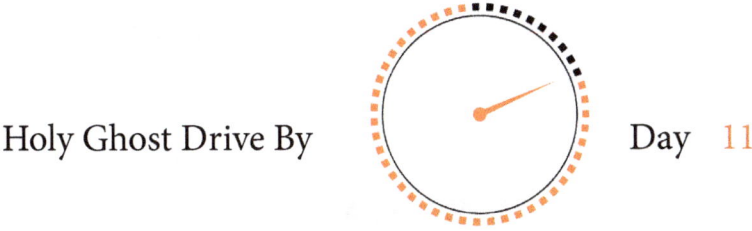 Day 11

When God is your source, you have a choice!

SEVERAL!!

Their help would be nice...but it will not be necessary.

Lock & Load

How does it feel knowing you have a choice?

Holy Ghost Drive By  Day 12

If they can not pick you up in the Spirit, flow with you in the Spirit and truly know your Spirit. Leave them out of ALL things *Spiritual!* What has been entrusted to you is too valuable to give access to the opportunistic novice.

They like to shine in your spotlight but will flee when you are given shade. For what you have been called to deal with, only the authentic can accompany you. Going forward, remember you do not need an *entourage*; you need *intercessors.*

Lock & Load

Who in your circle has offered to pray with/for you?

Who has God entrusted to you?

Is there anyone that agitates/irritates your soul?

Holy Ghost Drive By  Day 13

The Holy Spirit is like a metal detector in the right hands. He will detect where the confusion is coming from. Nothing stays hidden from Him. Lord, reveal it and remove it. Now, if you pray this prayer, do not focus on who *leaves*. Focus on the *peace* that remains.

Lock & Load

Write the prayer for today and the events that follow.

Holy Ghost Drive By  Day 14

I heard this morning, *"Take the brakes off!"* So many of us have put brakes on what God has given us, halting gifting and creativity, for fear of backlash from insecure people. If I do this, they might say this. If I share this, they might think I am showing off. If I start this, they might not support. If I do this, they might steal my idea.

Stop tripping, and start *producing!* Time is drawing near, and the hour is coming when no man can work. God has given you the keys to the kingdom. Your gifts and creativity unlock the closed doors. Work it!

They are going to talk about you if you do. They are going to talk about you if you do not. Haters will hate, but creators need to create.

You have too much in you
to be stagnat from fear.

Your financial freedom is in you and it must
be released. If they do not want it where you have been
marketing, then pray for a new circle of eager clientele.

God has provided receivers for what you have to offer.
He wants you rich in order to finance Kingdom
agendas. So go ahead and work while it is day
for when night cometh no man can work.

Lock & Load

What area of your life have you been holding back/hesitant?

Extra Clip: Greater is He that is in You, than he that is in the world.
1 John 4:4

TARGET  PRACTICE

Depression

> Which Holy Ghost Drive By did you aim at depression this week?

Procrastination

> How did you take out procrastination this week?

Fear

> How did you fight fear this week?

Holy Ghost Drive By  Day 15

True Story: Growing up, we lived in a neighborhood that was mostly Caucasian. I had some little friends who lived next door to us who always came to my yard to play, but I never was invited in their yard.

One day two of the little girls came over and asked my mom if my sister and I could come to their house and watch them swim. My mother asked,
"You mean can they come swim."

The little girl said, "No. We want them to watch us swim, not get in!!!"

My mother who was a strong, black, "We Are The People" type of woman said,
"Oh, no babies. My daughters know very well how to swim. There is no need for them to leave their home

to watch anybody swim!'"
Two weeks, later the pool company was at our house.

Moral of The Story: There are some people who invite you to be a spectator when you are the expert. It is what you are anointed and called to do. Your presence is their validation. Decline the invitation. You have not been called to validate
but to set the captives free.

There is no need to leave your home to watch others do, what you are made to do.
They do not want your participation but your influence, you are good, swim on!

Lock & Load

Have you been invited for your influence?

Holy Ghost Drive By  Day 16

Never mistake a *midwife* for a *nanny*.
The roles are totally different.

The *midwife* is there to coach you and tell you when to push in order to deliver whats in you. Once that is done their role is done.

The *nanny* is there to watch over
and help babysit your vision.
Both are necessary but different.

You will be hurt if you get the two confused.
The midwife moved on because the delivery was complete.

Lock & Load

Who around you nurtures your vision and holds you accountable?

Holy Ghost Drive By 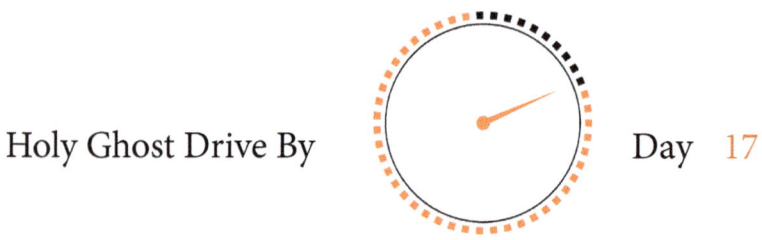 Day 17

They *knew* it was a lie when they heard it.
They chose to believe it to *avoid* obeying what God told them to do concerning you.

Do not worry He is correcting it.
They will apologize *and* obey with something extra **for the delay.**

Lock & Load

What blesssings are you in need of?

P.S. Do not gloat as you feast in
front of your enemies. Just thank them for the delivery

Holy Ghost Drive By 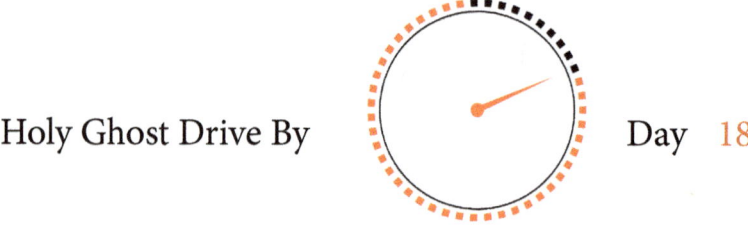 Day 18

When a *visionary* shows up, change is inevitable. They can see where the problem is, and they know how to recognize real help. The visionary does not stroke the problematic, but they encourage the *problem solvers.*

Stop stroking the hindrances and start supporting the help!

Lock & Load

How can you bless the ones that help you?

Holy Ghost Drive By  Day 19

Truth: There was a lady who came up to me after the play, *When Momma Prays*, and hugged me, she said I thought I knew you from radio
but I see I did not really know you.
It hit me hard in a good way.

The Lord said, many who thought they knew you handled you in the way they knew you, but as I unveil the many facets of you, some will be drawn but others will be driven away.

The ones who will be driven away will be the ones who benefited from you not knowing all of who you were.
They got their identity from your blind spots.
They needed you to need them.

In your pursuit of purpose,
you will not be able to pacify.

Those that know you in spirit will *adjust*, those that knew you in convenience and need will be *removed*.
Keep going and keep growing.
God has a need for the *real* you, all facets

Lock & Load

How does it feel to know God has a need for the real you?

Holy Ghost Drive By  Day 20

The vision is going to *speak* for you, close your mouth!

You do not have to justify what God has already qualified!

No matter who says no, you can not be denied.

If you heard no, you heard a lie.

God's resources are in unlimited supply.

Lock & Load

Write a poem of praise, thanking God for your yes.

Share your poem with me
JPBeasPro@gmail.com

Holy Ghost Drive By  Day 21

My key chain is weighed down by jiggling options! I only use three keys. The remaining clanking brass belongs to old places I no longer visit. I get frustrated when I am looking for a key to open a door.

It just dawned on me to just get rid of the ones that no longer work *duh!* Its hard to let go of things at times that once opened doors and gave you access. If you are bold enough to release them, your new keys will have room.

New access to new places will be granted!

Lock & Load

Which one of your habits is not serving your purpose?

TARGET  PRACTICE

Depression

Which Holy Ghost Drive By did you aim at depression this week?

Procrastination

How did you take out procrastination this week?

Fear

How did you fight fear this week?

Holy Ghost Drive By 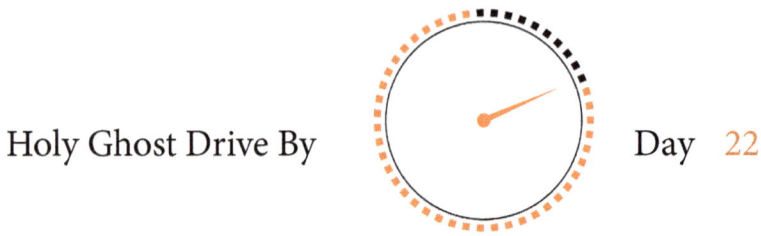 Day 22

Visionary: You were not even considered as a candidate, but your behind the scene dedication made you a commander.

Integrity and determination are door openers.
Do not throw away those keys.
They will open the right doors.

Lock & Load

What is waiting for you behind the door opened by integrity and determination?

Blessing or Curse

Holy Ghost Drive By  Day 23

The *determination* will outweigh the *depression*.
Put your focus on the greater for your latter shall be greater than your former.
What did not kill you built you.
You are stronger than you know and further along than you think.

Every underhanded scheme planned against you was revealed and demolished. You have unseen help.
Soon you will be shown victory in *everything* you put your hands to.

God has you covered from every direction.
You are energy that can not be contained.

Lock & Load

Draw your greater.

Holy Ghost Drive By  Day 24

I heard a word this morning.
It was a familiar word. Yet, it was so powerful to me this morning. I kept hearing the word, *understudy.*

As a producer and a playwright, I understand what understudies are. They are the prepared backup just in case the star of the role can not make it to production. The understudy prepares in the background just in case they are needed.
Years ago, while in production I opted against understudies. A week before the launch of the play, *When Momma Prays,* the leading actress announces that she can not make it.

A week before!!!!

I was in a full-blown panic, worrying about what to do?!

The grace of God sent a young lady my way that learned the role in three days and killed it!

God: I did that for you because you were unprepared. I will not do it again.

Your word: The understudies are ready!
The understudies are prepared!
Do not think you will not have to use an understudy. I learned from experience that the show must go on. I learned from experience to always have an understudy. There are some people waiting in the wings that are excited and ready to do what you have been begging somebody else to do.

Lock & Load

List the qualities your understudy *must* have.

Holy Ghost Drive By  Day 25

You have been hidden in plain sight.
Those who have insight
will see.

Stay ready!

Lock & Load

Seek God. Ask what are some reasons He will hide you?

Share your God experience
JPBeasPro@gmail.com

Holy Ghost Drive By  Day 26

It will be obvious.
They said you would not make it without them

Trying the Spirit by the Spirit:

That was a lie!

You have it in you!!

Lock & Load

List The Lies You Believed	Truth aka God's Word
Ex: You will be broke your whole life	Obedience elevates me from being a borrower to being a lender Deuteronomy 28:12

Lock & Load

List The Lies You Believed	Truth aka God's Word

Lock & Load

List The Lies You Believed	Truth aka God's Word

Holy Ghost Drive By  Day 27

Do not waste your platform.
In Esther 4, Mordecai told Esther about the plan to kill Jesus. He asked Esther to persuade the King not to order the genocide. Esther was reluctant, but Mordecai reminded her she was a Jew and could be killed too. He asked her *what if* this mission was the *purpose* of her position in the palace.

Where has God placed you to be a benefit to others? We can not ask God for promotion, and when He gives it, act brand new and unprepared.
We are only blessed to be a blessing.

Who can you open a door for or render favor to because you have been given authorization?

Do not waste your platform being prideful and selfish, because you were once in need of a favor. You too once needed someone to show you compassion.

Remember, the people you refuse to help today could very well be the people you need help from tomorrow.
Promotion neither cometh from the North, South, East or West but from God. He brings one up and another one down.

Whatever you do today, *DO NOT* waste your platform.

Lock & Load

How did you use your platform to bless someone today?

Share your God experience
JPBeasPro@gmail.com

Holy Ghost Drive By  Day 28

Your presence is a threat to the enemy. You can still show up for what he is trying to block you from! It may not be in person, but it can still be in power.

What made you say,
"Forget it. I'll just ride this out?"

In some cases, this ride is trying to take us to the grave. Jump *out* of the vehicle of stagnation and worry. Jump *in* the presence of God.

He is truly showing us another route to get to the Promised Land. Stay connected and stay determined.
We will get to the other side.

Oh, and you have time now to see who the

hitchhikers were. If your vehicle stalled and they are not trying to help you push, you now know.

Keep it *MOVING*!

Lock & Load

What is your passenger count?

Holy Ghost Drive By  Day 29

Holy Ghost boldness and authority.
Before you can even ask, it shall be granted!

What you sowed in *faith* and *sacrifice*
will be restored greater!

SWEATLESS VICTORIES!!

The enemies you once saw, you will see no more!!!

Lock & Load

What is the Lord pushing you to launch?

Holy Ghost Drive By   Day 30

There comes a time in your life that you no longer want the confinement of the crowd. You come into your own and say,
"I can not stay here any longer. I got places to go! People to meet and things to do!"

Lesson from the lepers sitting at the gate
(2 Kings 7:3-20)
They thought, 'If we stay here we will die. If we move, we may die. If we do nothing, we are going to die anyway! I do not know about you, but I gotta get up and get out!'

It is time to launch where He leads!
Let us go!!
I am rolling with or without a passenger.

Lock & Load

Celebrate!!

Take a moment and praise the Lord for the things He has done!!

Share your playlist with me!!
JPBeasPro@gmail.com

Holy Ghost Drive By  Day 31

Truth: 2019 was a year of unwanted growth. I was stretched in every area of my life, including mentally. The difficult part about this time was caring for my mom. I watched her health decline despite my prayers and efforts. Not to mention, I preached her homegoing service. While juggling all this, I did not miss a day of work.

I *kept* sowing and producing.

I took a trip to the mountains, and all I could do was cry! I wept like I had not wept in years.

It finally hit me just how *low* in the valley I was. I could not feel it because, in spite of the pain, I kept it moving even when I could not feel myself moving.

I *kept* encouraging when I needed encouragement the most.

I *kept* guiding even when I needed guidance the most.

I *kept* laughing when my circumstances were laughing at me.

Moral of the story: We will all have some valley experiences, but *keep* doing what you know to do. Stay close to Him always! No matter the twist and turns in the road, you will make it to the mountain!

The elevated view is not to look down on others, but to show them the *trail* that led you out of the *trial.* When you get to the mountain, do not forget to praise Him and seek Him more, because there are more valleys to go through.
At least you know now you are just passing through them. The same God who brought you over then is the same God who will bring you out NOW!

Last thing, never apologize for your mountain top experience because you fought all kinds of lions, tigers, and bears to get there!!!!!!

Lock & Load

How will you behave in the valley and on the mountain top?

Salvation Stop

Now it is time to offer you the best
ride you will ever have
in your life!

It is the *Holy Ghost* ride to salvation!
I can not promise you that you will
not hit some bumps and take some
curves on this journey. I can promise
you if you stay focused and stay in the
car you
will make it to the ultimate destination
Heaven!
You ready?

Let us ride. *Repeat after me:*
Lord Jesus, I know that I
am a sinner and I ask for your
forgiveness.
I believe you died for my sins and rose
from the dead.
I turn from my sins and invite you to

come into my heart and life. I want to trust you as my Lord and Savior! Today, Lord I receive you into my heart and confess with my mouth you are my Lord and savior!
Today and forever, I am saved!!

Congratulations!

If you prayed that prayer, please let us know so we can officially celebrate your decision! Welcome to the family!!!

Let us know!
www.JBProductions.work

Congratulations!!!

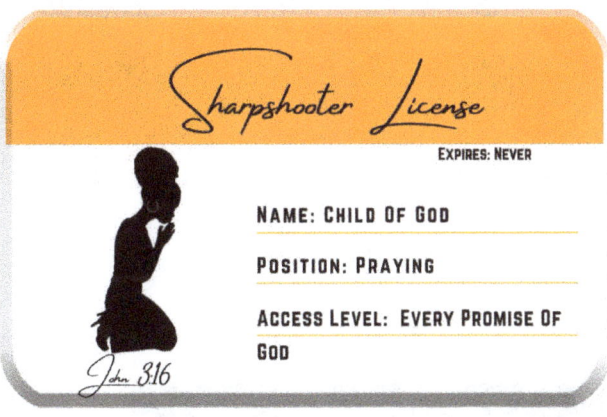

I hereby certify you to use God's Word to shoot down every attack of the enemy!

Stay Tuned In With Sharpshooter

Jerri P. Beasley

Download Our App

Be on the look out for Jerri P. Beasley's Hit stage play, "When Momma Prays" in your city!

www.ingramcontent.com/pod-product-compliance
Lightning Source LLC
Chambersburg PA
CBHW070937160426
43193CB00011B/1718